THE FARNSWORTH HOUSE

Franz Schulze

Produced by Lohan Associates
Designer, David Salvia
Project editor, William Huchting
Cover photograph by George Lambros
Typefaces, Avenir Book and Avenir Black
ISBN 0-9660840-0-4

THE FARNSWORTH HOUSE

I pointed out to him [Mies] that it [a glass house] was impossible because you had to have rooms, and that meant solid walls up against the glass, which ruined the whole point.

Mies said, "I think it can be done."

—Philip Johnson, speaking at a symposium held at the School of Architecture, Columbia University, 1961

The House, First View

Part of the prestige of the Farnsworth House rests upon the renown of the man who designed it, Ludwig Mies van der Rohe, by consensus one of the several most illustrious architects of the twentieth century. Yet Mies's own reputation derives in no small degree from the excellence of the building itself and the high place it holds in the history of modern residential architecture.

The most obvious and exceptional fact about the Farnsworth House is that it is a single space walled from floor to ceiling in glass. Only a few other houses have been similarly composed, most notably Philip Johnson's Glass House in New Canaan, Connecticut, which was finished in 1949, fully two years prior to the completion of the Farnsworth House. But Johnson freely acknowledges that he got the idea for his own design only after making an enthralled examination of the plans Mies had begun as early as 1946. The Farnsworth House is, in short, the first of an extraordinary building type as well as an unsurpassed example of it.

Most viewers are arrested by their initial perception of the house. The disarmingly simple rectilinear geometry of its white piers and slabs creates an impression, which Mies fully intended, of architectural structure reduced to an abstracted essence, with the resultant image all the more striking as seen against the backdrop of a wooded natural environment. Closer inspection reveals that the floor of the house is constructed at a level some five feet above the ground. There is a practical reason for this. The proximity of the Fox River, which flows westerly a few yards away from the south elevation, is a reminder that this is a flood plain; the house is set high enough to ride above encroaching water. Yet on account of this very sense of lift, visually heightened by the white of the painted steel, the house seems in a state of levitation, and the

visitor is prompted to the plausible conclusion that the architect was moved as much by esthetic as by functional considerations in siting and constructing the building as he did. This sense is progressively reinforced, first, by the distinction between the palpable sturdiness of the steel structure and the apparent immateriality of the glass walls it frames, second, by the artful but eminently clear route of access. The house is built on a rectangular plan with an east-west longitudinal axis, its floor slab and roof slab fixed and supported by eight wide-flange piers, four to each of the long sides. The main structure is made up of the glass-enclosed living area to the east, and an open, roofed deck to the west. Approach is dictated by the presence of a spacious terrace, oriented south and slightly west, that intervenes between grade and the floor level of the main structure. One stair leads from the ground to the terrace, another thence to the deck, where a right-hand

Right: The Farnsworth House's smooth white steel frame hovers over the flood plain.

Below: An early design of the house rendered in watercolor, shown above a photograph of Philip Johnson's Glass House. The Glass House bears striking similarity to some of Mies's preliminary design for the Farnsworth House, in particular, the cylindrical core and the cabinets of the interior.

Bottom: The south, north and east elevations testify to the marked simplicity of the structure.

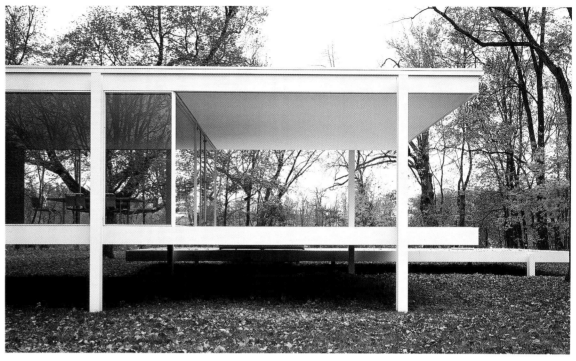

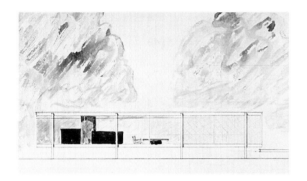

turn, eastward, is called for in order to reach the double entry door.

Just as the visible exterior form is minimally expressed, the space within is kept maximally open. The principal activating element of the interior is a compact wood-lined core situated slightly closer to the north wall of the structure than to the south, with a space between each of its ends and the outer walls. The core, sheathed in rich primavera wood, contains a kitchen facility to the north, a utility room flanked by two bathrooms east and west, and a sitting area to the south. Plumbing, wiring and circulation fans are embedded in a cylindrical stack inside the utility room. This division of function creates a flowing system of unpartitioned but definable zones: the sitting area, or parlor, dominant in its size and addressed by a panelled wall with a fireplace recessed within the core; the kitchen, which connects with a dining area west of the core; and a sleeping area east of the core. The last of these

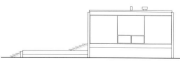

spaces is served by a free-standing, teak-clad storage closet.

It is in the interior that the full impact of Mies's expressive objectives is most clearly felt. For there the dialogue of tangible, reductivist structure and intangible, open space, each dependent on the other, is asserted with unqualified clarity. No sooner is this evident than the view of the outdoors imposes itself, alluring to behold and constantly shifting according to weather conditions, time of day or the changing seasons. The house provides shelter by filtering nature rather than by walling it off. Mies's own reflections confirm this: "When one looks at Nature through the glass walls of the Farnsworth House," he once said, "it takes on a deeper significance than when one stands outside. More of Nature is thus expressed—it becomes part of a greater whole."A similar sentiment was recalled by a guest who once spent the night in the house: "The sleeping area is to the east, where the sun rises. The sensation is indescribable—the act of waking and coming to consciousness as the light dawns and gradually grows. It illuminates the grass and trees and the river beyond; it takes over your whole vision. You are in nature and not in it, engulfed by it but separate from it. It is altogether unforgettable."

Nature is thus integral to the viewer's comprehension of the architecture. The seven acres of the original narrow strip of land on which Mies was commissioned to build are themselves laid out in an east-west direction bordering the low banks of the river. In choosing the exact site for the house, Mies was moved to situate it behind and in the shade of the district's most venerable black sugar maple tree, once, at the turn of the 1950s, resplendent and now slowly dying, but still majestic, a foil to the geometry of the architecture and a screen through which the river is visible. During the autumn it turns a radiant gold, underscoring further the contrast of the flat white of the house with its variegated setting.

This interplay of colors and textures led the current owner, Lord Peter Palumbo of London, to assign the task of landscaping the Farnsworth grounds to the late Lanning Roper, an American who lived in

Right: The core and the storage closet act as partitions, creating the sleeping and sitting areas. Note the hopper window on the left.

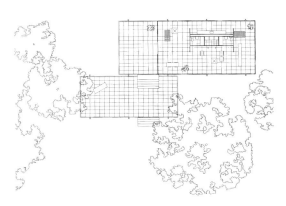

England. In its earlier state, when its original owner, Dr. Edith Farnsworth, occupied it, the house looked out east, north and west on terrain filled with grassland, natural scrub and a scattering of trees. In 1972 Roper, a devotee of the traditional, informally planned English garden, planted trees east and west, leaving the space directly behind and north of the house to a tract of lawn that slopes lazily upward toward River Road. This open space he filled with daffodils, literally tens of thousands of them, which blossom progressively in the spring, leaving the ground decorated with patches of dappled yellow and white. The moment of bloom is brief but compelling, and the landscape hardly less attractive

later, when the flowers give way to a meadow wholly of summery green. Meanwhile, Roper's stands of trees west, north and east provide not only an enclosure for the house but the natural *mise-en-scène* that Mies granted such importance in his aforementioned remarks.

Critical opinion over the near half century of the house's existence has been marked by a steady stream of praise of the highest order. Kenneth Frampton: "a work of metaphysical beauty." Reyner Banham: "[The house] left other architects little to do except to try to make even more perfect that which was already perfected."

The Architect

Mies van der Rohe was born in 1886 in Aachen, once the capital of Charlemagne's empire, later a thriving provincial city in the newly consolidated German Empire. While his rearing in a family of stonemasons bred a respect for the crafts that never left him, his desire to become an architect was fed by the rapid industrialization of his homeland during the mid- to late 19th century. Mies received no formal architectural training, learning the practice of building instead as an apprentice on construction sites around Aachen and as a draftsman in several local architects' offices, where he displayed a striking gift for drawing that led him to seek a higher calling in Berlin.

Following a brief assistantship with the architect-designer Bruno Paul, he built his first independent work, a suburban house in Potsdam, in 1907, before deciding a year later to refine his technical skills by joining the office of Peter Behrens, then one of the several leading architects in Germany. Behrens's fame rested largely on the innovative work he had done for the German electrical industry, but it was his admiration for the great 19th century neoclassicist Karl Friedrich Schinkel that left the deepest mark on his young associate. Mies shortly produced another independent scheme, the monumental Kröller-Müller House project of 1912, conceived in a neo-classical, Schinkelesque style. Intended for The Hague but never built, it was demonstrably the most ambitious of his pre-World War I endeavors.

After the war, Mies spent several years, until 1921, producing no actual architecture but moving in the circles of the rapidly developing modernist

Top left: Mies as a young man, 1912.

Bottom left: Schinkel's Gardener's Cottage at Schloss Charlottenhof, near Potsdam. "When I came as a young man to Berlin and looked around, I was interested in Schinkel because Schinkel was the most important architect in Berlin.... I studied him carefully and came under his influence.... I think Schinkel had wonderful constructions, excellent proportions, and good details."—Mies van der Rohe in an interview with Peter Blake, 1960

Top right: The Riehl House of 1907, Potsdam: Mies's interest in the relationship between building and landscape is apparent in his first built work.

Center right: Model of the Kröller-Müller project of 1912.

Bottom right: The plan of one of Mies's most famous theoretical studies, the Brick Country House of 1924.

culture of Berlin, where he absorbed influences that amounted arguably to the most important of his career. Among these was one of the central tenets of modernism, namely that the advanced visual arts could reach a deeper expressive level by probing beneath the surface of 19th century descriptive naturalism in painting and the historicist ornamental overlay common to 19th century architecture. This search for essences was conducted by the process of abstraction, the stripping away of all that presumably concealed the Truth, to put it in typically Miesian terms, lying at the vital center. In a journal published in the early 1920s by Mies and his Berlin colleagues (called *G*, for *Gestaltung*, roughly the English equivalent of form-giving), the revealing term they applied to their activities was *elementar*, identical in meaning with its cognate in English: elemental, or fundamental.

Beginning with 1921, Mies turned away from all reference to historical styles, maintaining contact with the past only by favoring a clarity of form and a rationality of expression traceable in large part to Schinkel and by choosing a stern geometric abstraction as the most fitting vehicle for the accomplish-

ment of his ends. Notwithstanding occasional variations over the years, these generalizations apply to virtually all his achievements of the 1920s, including five spectacular, unrealized but immensely influential projects for high-rise buildings and houses (1921–24); the supervision of a widely publicized collection of buildings in the new modernist manner, the Weissenhof Housing Colony in Stuttgart (1927); and his two individual European masterworks, studies in lucidity of structure and openness of space, the German Pavilion of the 1929 International Exposition in Barcelona and the Tugendhat House in Brno (1928-30). Moreover, while the Nazi accession of 1933 led at last to his decision to emigrate to the U.S. in 1938, none of his work during or following the 1930s veered from the qualities most identified with him: precision and integrity of form carried out, as often as possible, in the most patrician of building materials.

The fact is, Mies did not invent the two phrases for which he is most famous: "Less is more" and "God is in the details," both of which are commonplaces reaching back well into history. On the other hand, a motto he did cite frequently not only

Top left and center: The German Pavilion of the 1929 International Exposition in Barcelona was extolled by Mies's former employer, the architect and industrial designer Peter Behrens, as the building that "will someday be hailed as the most beautiful ... of the twentieth century." The Pavilion was demolished soon after the Exposition closed.

Above: Mies's Tugendhat House, Brno, Czech Republic. Much of the furniture in the Farnsworth House was originally designed for the Tugendhat House.

belongs to him, and probably him alone, but also pertains more precisely than the other axioms to his architectural goals. "Beinahe nichts," or, literally, "almost nothing," is a poetic characterization, brief in itself, of the understated ends and means of his European and American work alike, especially of the latter.

His American period, indeed, is famous for the time and energy he spent on a building type appropriate to the reductivism of structure and space implicit in the creative goal of "almost noth-ing": the one-story clear-span pavilion. Among his most famous American works are Crown Hall (1956) and the National Gallery of Berlin (1968), the former housing the school of architecture he himself headed at Illinois Institute of Technology after he moved from Berlin to Chicago in 1938, the latter a museum of modern art serving the once and future German capital. These buildings and several like them from the American years are notable for the breadth and width of their column-free interior spaces, an attribute made architecturally feasible by ceilings suspended from trusses, girders or two-way frames. The openness of the space is thus a consequence of the attention paid the supporting structure, with the freedom of one dependent on the clarity of the other. The commingling of space and structure has already been cited here as among the most telling features of the Farnsworth House. While it is much smaller than Mies's famous commercial and institutional American clear-span buildings, its dates (1946–51) certify its place among their earliest realized antecedents, and one of the most exquisitely executed.

The Client

According to the most credible reports, Mies was introduced to Edith Farnsworth sometime in the winter of 1945–46 at a dinner party on Chicago's North Side. Farnsworth, 42 at the time, was a nephrologist at Chicago's Passavant Memorial Hospital whose reputation as a researcher was growing in the the national medical community. Mies was 59, already renowned within the international architectural world, yet still relatively little known to the American public.

Farnsworth herself was hardly unaware of him. As a woman of exceptional learning and intelligence, she remained steadily informed about artistic as well as scientific matters. Some of the Asian art she collected became part of the permanent collection of the Art Institute of Chicago. In the course of her first conversation with Mies, she mentioned that she had in mind building a weekend house for herself on property she owned close by the Fox River, near Plano, some sixty miles west of Chicago. Might someone in his office be interested in such an assignment?

Mies allowed he might be interested himself. While much of his reputation rested on residences he had designed in Europe, he had never had the opportunity to complete a house in the U.S., and the prospect seized his attention. He and Farnsworth promptly agreed to visit the site together and the commission followed.

The personal relationship between Mies and Farnsworth is a story engaging unto itself, moreover inseparable from the history of the house as a work of architectural significance. Farnsworth was single

Edith Farnsworth as a young intern at Passavant Memorial Hospital, Chicago.

and, by her own confession, a bored and lonely woman. Mies, though legally married, had left his wife and family in Europe long before he emigrated, and he now lived a life free of conventional marital ties.

Thus there were grounds for a bond of sorts, although it took a while before factors more inherently divisive made themselves felt. Mies was a man of great personal charm and attractiveness to women, but his ferociously inward-turned dedication

to his work discouraged any lasting intimate personal relationships. Farnsworth, whose formidable intellect compensated, but never enough, for a tall and ungainly physical presence, was as eager for companionship as Mies was indifferent to it except as it served, or in no way interfered with, his creative purposes.

While the house brought them together, then, it was always one thing to her, quite another to him. If it offered her surcease from weekend isolation in the city, and even better, a stimulating and potentially enduring relationship with a man of elegance and immense professional distinction, it provided him— since it was a bachelor's country retreat little burdened by customary domestic necessities—the uncommon opportunity to create a purified realization of the minimalist form ("almost nothing") that he associated with his most serious artistic aspirations.

For a while Mies and Farnsworth worked superbly together. He was the dominant partner, but she was fully equal to understanding, and appreciating, the potentially historic significance of the project. She visited his office frequently and both of them convened from time to time for picnics at the Fox River site. Halcyon months passed. Left to his own devices, Mies was by nature scrupulously slow at his business, and Farnsworth saw less reason to press him than to grant him the time and space he seemed to need—which in any case secured more of him for herself. Not until later did a rift open between them and deepen finally into a gulf so wide it could be bridged only by the courts, where a long, bitter legal battle left him the material victor, both of them the spiritual losers.

The House, Design Phase

Despite Mies's normally deliberate working method, he was surprisingly quick in arriving at the basic form of the house. By the end of 1946, the plan had been fixed, with the main enclosure meant to be bracketed and supported by six externally profiled columns and the deck by two, with floor, roof and terrace slabs cantilevered east and west. The terrace would be situated as now, with one stair reaching it from the ground, another rising from its surface to that of the deck. (In several early sketches a second stair is shown leading from the ground to the north edge of the terrace.) While Mies's long-standing reputation as a classicist is borne out in early and late stages by the axiality of the glazed enclosure and deck, he could deviate at will from doctrinaire classicism—much the way his hero Schinkel freely employed asymmetries in his Italianate villas in Potsdam near Berlin. The very location of the Farnsworth terrace ajog of the house attests to this. A similar informality in the interior is evident from the outset, with the core invariably shown closer to the northeast corner of the house than to the lateral axis.

With only few exceptions, variations in the preliminary plans are restricted to the treatment of interior space. A model constructed for inclusion in the 1947 Museum of Modern Art retrospective of Mies's work had the deck enclosed in screening. Some of the several hundred preliminary drawings show a second sleeping area proposed in the northwest quadrant, a space eventually given over to the dining area. The core was subjected to assorted shifts, in some instances appearing too short to accommodate two bathrooms, in others showing walls not deep enough to make room for a fireplace. There is even one curious suggestion of a pair of glass partitions that would have connected the core to mullions on the north wall, thus interrupting the spatial circulation otherwise so essential to the final open interior space. It seems safe to presume that such notions were mostly fragmentary evidence of Mies's restless pursuit of ideas and solutions. On occasion he could

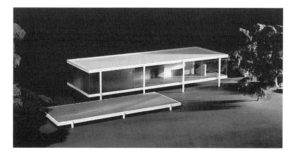

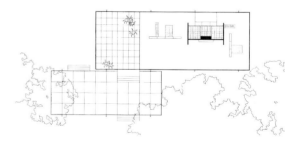

Top: The entry eventually had doors that are slightly off center, subtly emphasizing the main sitting area. Mies worked within a grid but made visual adjustments.

Above, left: The model shown at the Museum of Modern Art in an exhibition of 1947.

Above, right: An early scheme: note the different size of the floor grids, the two separate sets of stairs rising to the terrace and the pair of glass screens partitioning the kitchen from the rest of the house.

Far right: Architect Myron
Goldsmith, Mies's assistant
on the Farnsworth House,
confers with Edith
Farnsworth.

Near right: The vertical
section illustrates the
fundamental design
elements: floor and roof are
hung from a wide-flange
pier, allowing for an
uninterrupted enclosure
of glass.

Below: Water that
infiltrates the porous
travertine is drained
through gravel-filled catch
basins underneath the floor.

Bottom: The lateral and
longitudinal sections
illustrate the differing
heights of the core and
wardrobe.

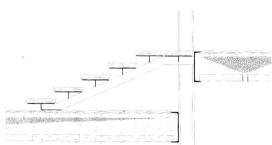

be exceedingly subtle, even too subtle for the functional good of the house. Virtually all the published drawings of the plan erroneously indicate the entry door symmetrically placed between the north and south walls. The fact is, it is closer to the south wall by about half the width of one of the travertine slabs that serve as modules of the floor surface. This seems a cunningly muted way of directing the attention of the visitor to the main sitting area, moreover, of implicitly defining a slightly larger space for the dining area. On the other hand, the decision to minimize the detailing of the fireplace area—a further sign of the devotion to "almost nothing"—freed that space of a defined hearth. Fires lit even from logs lying on a makeshift hearth had the unhappy effect of creating a wild circulation of ash throughout the interior. Dirk Lohan, the architect (and Mies's grandson) who discovered this condition when he was later charged with the restoration of the house, decided to correct it by installing an enclosing platform made of the same travertine. Edith Farnsworth, he suspected, only rarely used the fireplace.

Another convenience she certifiably did without was air conditioning. A modicum of cross ventilation could be achieved by opening the entry doors to the west and a pair of hopper windows on the east window wall, with a modest flowage added by activating a fan set in the floor slab of the house and

drawing warm air downward to the ground, thus avoiding the visual impediment of an air conditioning unit. Mies's desire to minimize the intrusion of ducts and pipes into the architectural expression is also apparent in the utilities stack. Painted black, it is visible on the exterior only to someone who stoops to make it out in the five-foot-high space separating house from ground. As for the extent, if any, to

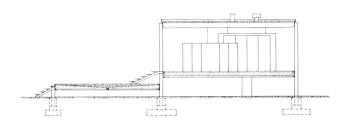

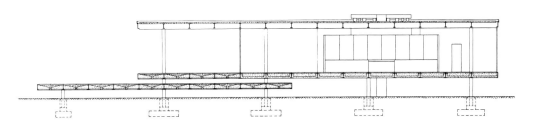

Below: Edith Farnsworth had screens fabricated for the deck, consistent with the model shown at the Museum of Modern Art in 1947. Chinese sculptures, of lions, are seen on the terrace to the right of the tree.

Left: The deck today.

Bottom: The heating and ventilation system, submarine-like in its compactness, is tucked away behind a hinged panel in the guest bathroom shower.

which that esthetic severity caused Edith Farnsworth distress, it is worth remembering that even well-to-do people of the Middle West in the late 1940s were long accustomed to enduring summer heat in their own homes. Air-conditioning in private dwellings was as much a rarity as it was a luxury. So far as is known, she was not troubled by the lack of it.

Heating and drainage were more unconditional necessities, and in both respects the Farnsworth House was and remains quite adequately equipped. Hot water pipes in a coil system embedded in the floor not only radiate heat throughout the interior but provide special comfort to feet chilled by the winter cold. The slowness of such a system to make itself felt to anyone entering the house when the heat has been turned off is alleviated by a small forced-air furnace in the utility room, whose fan blows a measure of warmth directly into the interior.

The solution of the problem of drainage, especially as it affected the floor of the deck and the terrace, is credited mostly to Mies's chief assistant on the Farnsworth project, Myron Goldsmith, who later went on to a distinguished career of his own. While most of the water simply runs off the travertine surface of the terrace, that which infiltrates the porous marble drains into a system of gravel-filled, sheet-metal pans welded into an inverted pyramid and then out through pipe openings to the ground. The flat roof, in turn, is bordered by low, single-beveled coping that water cannot overflow before draining into a central pipe, directly above the core, that is connected to the utility room stack.

The House, Construction Phase

The considerable length of time that separated the commission and the completion of the house—five years—is explained only partially by Mies's deliberateness in refining details. He was in fact prepared to begin construction by the end of 1947. It was Farnsworth who had to wait until 1949 to receive money from an inheritance that enabled her to approve the actual start of building.

Largely because the frame was a self-supporting steel structure, it went up rather quickly. The eight wide-flange columns, resting on concrete footings, were welded flush to the fascias of floor and roof, with the latter two elements made up of girders crossing laterally, with diagonal bracing, and finally filled in with concrete. Photographs taken during construction attest to the simplicity of the skeleton, although the completed house is a remarkably straightforward realization of Mies's fundamental structural idea. The Farnsworth House is one of the first completed buildings in which the architect made use of the wide-flange steel beam that became so crucial a component of the architectural vocabulary of his American years. The economy of this steel shape speaks for itself, although one of his assistants in the design and construction of the house, Gene

Top, and bottom right: The steel structure. "To me, structure is something like logic. It is the best way to do things and to express them. I am very skeptical about emotional expressions. I don't trust them, and I don't think they will last for long."—Mies, in a 1960 interview with Peter Blake.

Above: A plumber, crouching in front of the flue that hangs from the ceiling, installs the hot water pipes which radiate heat through the floor slab.

Summers, has suggested that Mies appreciated the beam not just for its constructive strength—a tube would have been stronger—but for its vigorously sculptural look and the tectonic character its placement on the exterior of the slabs added to the structure. In short, the wide-flange beam spoke to his esthetic sense as surely as it represented the steel technology he so often claimed as a point of departure in his work. A sympathy with the crafts that dated from his childhood further prompted him to have the frame sandblasted smooth and painted white rather than left rough. Moreover, he depended greatly on the services of a local wood craftsman, Karl Freund, in the fabrication of the primavera of the core that endowed the whole interior with such an atmosphere of warmth. Mies himself, son of a stone-

mason, devoted himself to no single phase more diligently than to the selection of the 24-by-33-inch slabs that make up the modules of the floor of the house and terrace. Travertine was one of Mies's favorite stones, and he employed it with singular effectiveness in the Farnsworth House. Even now, the slabs, white tinged with gray and all of them original, remain among the features most immediately arresting to the visitor.

The final phase of the construction, which took place in the summer of 1951, after Farnsworth had moved into the house, consisted of the construction of a screen around the deck, a device inspired by the swarms of mosquitoes that infested the Fox River valley in the summer months. By most accounts, Mies was never happy with the idea of a screen, even

though his consent to it early on was evident in the 1947 model shown at the Museum of Modern Art. Since nothing like it was included in the building as he completed it, we may presume it was Farnsworth who finally saw it through, and only after the good will had vanished from her relationship with Mies. She assigned the task to an assistant in Mies's office, William Dunlap, who carried it out under slightly awkward circumstances, with Mies regularly visiting his Chicago residence, offering advice, then beating a hasty departure when he heard Farnsworth coming.

As finished, the screen was built on a steel framework that included a mullion at each of the west corners of the deck, and a pair of doorways side by side along the south elevation, each opening on a central pivot.

Architect versus Client

The order and importance of the factors that ruptured the relationship between Mies and Farnsworth have been obscured with the passage of time. There were plenty of practical issues, ranging from serious ones, like disagreements over the cost of the house and disappointments over its function, to trivialities, including an argument over the selection of a color for the draperies. Less precisely measurable but surely of substantial consequence were the similarities in their personalities qualified by the differences in their emotional priorities. Since both were driven by exceptionally strong wills and motives of high seriousness, the force that brought them together was of comparable magnitude, moreover equal to the one that finally drove them apart. If it is simplistic to say that Farnsworth wanted the house and Mies, and Mies wanted the house and the next client, such a summation comes as close to the heart of the matter as any other, and maybe closer. In a chapter of her unpublished memoirs, a reference to "My Mies-conception" was followed by a litany of complaints: The roof leaked. Excessive condensation formed on the window-walls. "Mies talks about his 'free space': but his space is very fixed. I can't even put a clothes hanger in my house without considering how it affects everything from the outside." In turn, Mies was heard to say, apparently in response to Farnsworth's criticisms, that she should "stick to her nephritis."

In the early days neither of them would have behaved so brutally toward the other. She knew his intentions well enough from the start and

Two letters from Edith Farnsworth to Mies. The business-like tone of the second hints at the chill that developed between them.

approved them, while he treated her, if not lovingly, with the respect and consideration a distinguished and valued client deserved. It is hard to avoid speculating that arguments over money and other practicalities were more nearly the results of an affective conflict than the causes of it. The evidence suggests that she yearned to find a friend, not just an architect. Less certain is whether she wanted more than that. Did she know that Mies had relationships of a more or less romantic nature with other women during the very years he was working on her house? Did this not matter to a woman who, recalling the evening she first discussed the house with Mies, reported that "the effect was tremendous, like a storm, a flood, or other act of God," and who early on judged his efforts as "such work one can only recognize and cherish—with love and respect"? Were the budgetary and functional problems that developed

over five years serious enough by themselves to alter her assessment of Mies at last as "simply colder and more cruel than anybody I have ever known," adding that "perhaps it was never a friend and an collaborator, so to speak, that he wanted, but a dupe and a victim"?

Whatever the underlying reasons, hostilities finally reached a point at which Mies sued Farnsworth, claiming she owed him money, and she countersued him, alleging he had overcharged her while falsely representing himself as "a skilled, proficient and experienced architect." A tedious, at times ruthless court trial ensued, dragging on until mid-1953, when the two of them, at great expense of spirit to both, settled in Mies's favor.

Nor did the matter end there. The newspapers made the most of the story of a major architect in conflict with a well-known client over a famous house, while the architectural press spun a political

The kitchen interior image contains the following article reproduction:

Something is rotten in the state of design—and it is spoiling some of our best efforts in modern living. After watching it for several years, after meeting it with silence, House Beautiful has decided to speak out and appeal to your common sense, because it is common sense that is mostly under attack. Two ways of life stretch before us. One leads to the richness of variety, to comfort and beauty. The other, the one we want fully to expose to you, retreats to poverty and unlivability. Worst of all, it contains a threat of cultural dictatorship

THE THREAT

TO THE NEXT AMERICA

By Elizabeth Gordon, *Editor*

Left: The kitchen during Edith Farnsworth's period of residence.

Above: The title page of the article in *House Beautiful* by Elizabeth Gordon. A sampling: "I have talked to a highly intelligent, now disillusioned, woman who spent more than $70,000 building a 1-room house that is nothing but a glass cage on stilts."

web around the issue, and no less grand an architectural figure than Frank Lloyd Wright provoked things further. In an article entitled "The Threat to the Next America," written at the height of the McCarthy/communist scare and published in the April 1953 issue of *House Beautiful*, Elizabeth Gordon wrote: "There is a well-established movement in modern architecture, decorating and furnishings which is promoting the mystical idea that 'less is more'...if we can be sold on accepting dictators in matters of taste and how our homes are to be ordered, our minds are certainly well prepared to accept dictators in other departments of life." Wright had more to say: "These Bauhaus architects [with whom Wright now identified Mies] ran from political totalitarianism in Germany to what is now made by specious promotion to seem their own totalitarianism in art here in America.... Why do I distrust and defy such 'internationalism' as I do communism? Because both must by their nature do this very leveling in the name of civilization."

Some years earlier, when Mies emigrated to the U.S., he and Wright enjoyed profound mutual respect and genuine friendship. Now both affections were lost to both men. To be sure, Mies remained steadfastly committed to his belief in the Farnsworth House, but people who knew him tend to the view that the overall unpleasantness of the experience caused him to reduce his commitment to further residential design in favor of commercial and institutional architecture, fields in which he went on to ever greater distinction in any case. Farnsworth, meanwhile, her fury vented repeatedly in the press, remained inwardly disconsolate. In her memoirs, she wrote: "The alienation which I feel today must have had its beginnings on that shady river bank all too soon abandoned by the herons which flew away to seek their lost seclusion farther upstream."

Farnsworth: Last Stand

Farnsworth's implicit identification of her sorry state with the flight of the herons was touched with poetic license. She did not, in fact, seek her own seclusion elsewhere, but remained in the house for nearly two decades, at one point even striking an uncompromisingly proprietary position toward it. Moreover, assuming the birds did take wing on account of the strange new structure that invaded their habitat, it is probable that they were moved more by its presence than by their opinion of its architectural quality. On a later occasion they had more to flee from than a house, and she more cause to sympathize with them. In the late 1960s the Board of Supervisors of Kendall County decided to widen the road leading south from Plano and the old single-lane bridge that carried it over the Fox River. Worse still, from Edith's standpoint, the new road and bridge would be moved to the east, where it would be all too visible from her property.

While intelligence and erudition were Farnsworth's most distinguishing qualities, her best friends knew her also as a feisty soul who did not shrink from a fight. Mies himself could testify to that. So could the Kendall County authorities, who, encountering her resistance to the new road plan, must have been impressed as much by her resourcefulness as by her tenacity. Well aware that

the road and bridge would be built over the northwest corner of her property, moreover, that the county had a nearly unassailable right of eminent domain, she contested the proposal anyhow, taking the matter to court and claiming that the construction would invade an ancient and sacred burial ground of the Fox tribe.

A generation or two later, such an argument might have carried some weight with the law. In 1967 it did not; she lost that case too. The road bed was shifted as planned and a bridge was built to accommodate it, both of them interfering with the theretofore untrammeled view from her house to the south. Thus it remains today.

Top: The main sitting area during Edith Farnsworth's residence. Note the fireplace and the lack of a defined hearth.

Bottom: The original bridge. The stone piers are all that remain today, standing to the west of the new bridge.

Opposite: The informality of Edith Farnsworth's furnishings contrasts with the formality of Mies's architecture.

The New Ownership

When Peter Palumbo was a schoolboy at Eton, a teacher who lectured regularly on art history showed him and his fellow students a picture of a building by the famous architect Mies van der Rohe. Palumbo remembered being smitten by it on first sight. It was the Farnsworth House. The name of the architect stayed with him; less so, the name of the house.

Much later, in the early 1960s, after he had reached manhood and gained fame as a real estate developer, he conceived the idea of putting up a major office building on a parcel of land he owned in London. He offered the commission to Mies, who accepted it. In the course of the next several years the two men met from time to time at the architect's offices in Chicago. On one such occasion, conversing with Mies's grandson Dirk Lohan, Palumbo remarked that he would be pleased to have Mies design not only the London building, but a house for himself, in Great Britain.

Knowing that his grandfather, in his late 70s and ailing, was obliged to husband his strength, Lohan observed that the Farnsworth House itself was for sale. Sometime in 1968 Palumbo paid a call on Edith Farnsworth in Plano, where it was agreed that he would make the purchase. She remained in residence until 1971, a year before

Palumbo took physical possession of a work of high art that he had dreamed about since he was a boy.

The new owner set a task for himself of not only restoring the house to its original condition but outfitting it with furnishings that would be truer to the architect's intentions than those Farnsworth put in place following the now famous breakup. Mies, whose reputation as a furniture designer was unsurpassed among the moderns,

had hoped early in the relationship with Farnsworth to design furniture specially for her house. It would have been the first he ever designed for a specific venue in America, and its failure to materialize may be among the saddest losses of the whole sad affair. In any case, his death in 1969 rendered the matter academic. Palumbo's decision to use examples of the famous furniture Mies designed around 1930 was consoling enough, given the ageless beauty of the

Right: Lord Peter Palumbo, shown here, fulfilled a dream when he purchased the Farnsworth House. An avid collector of art, Palumbo displays many pieces from his collection at the house, such as this untitled sculpture by Harry Bertoia (opposite).

chairs, ottomans, tables and lounge that, along with several objects designed by the architect Dirk Lohan, continue to grace the Farnsworth interior today.

Otherwise, the new owner was content to leave the house pretty much alone. He installed air conditioning by concealing a unit above the core, removed the screen wall from around the deck, hung natural-colored draperies on the windows, and directed the refinishing of the primavera, which had darkened to an unsightly brown over the years. An even more avid collector of art than Farnsworth, most of it from the twentieth century, he limited the objects shown in the house to free-standing sculpture, thus abiding by Mies's explicit recommendations not to hang pictures on the wood panels of the core.

In some senses he is the ideal owner of the place, not least because his reverence for Mies has only grown over the years. Since he maintains his primary residence in London, he is able to make use of the house as a retreat, which is what it was meant to be in the first place. Nor has that pre-vented him from regularly bringing his family there, including children. On such occasions informality reigns, with the young ones cheerfully passing the night in sleeping bags on the floor of the sitting area. Further to this, Palumbo and his wife Hayat have found the house altogether suitable for themselves as a couple, since the living, dining, kitchen and sleeping spaces are sufficiently inter-flowing to encourage companionship, sufficiently separated to allow individual privacy.

The principal alterations have been made to the landscape, where Palumbo worked closely with Lanning Roper to effect the aforementioned changes in the plantings. Since before selling the property Farnsworth added 55 acres to her original seven, Palumbo has occasionally placed outdoor sculptures throughout the area. The grounds remain informally cast, reinforcing the notion that the house is dependent on its natural environment. Hayat Palumbo has been especially mindful of the drama that constantly plays between shelter and setting: "The sunrise, of course, is ravishing. But the night as well, especially during thunderstorms. Snowfalls are magical. And I recall times when the river water rose almost to the level of the floor, but not quite, so that we had to locomote by canoe. The house became a marina. I cannot recall a dull moment here."

The River

Hayat Palumbo's recollections of the watery wonderland occasionally surrounding the Farnsworth House have had an historical downside that has grown from afterthought to major concern. In the early stages of design, Mies's office made inquiry into the history of the flooding that was a regular occurrence on the property. Government records were consulted and even local citizens interviewed, in a thorough effort to determine the record of the highest floods of the previous hundred years. The answer, three feet, led Mies to lift the floor of the house to a level two feet higher than that.

It proved a perfect way to tempt fate. In 1954, just three years after Edith Farnsworth moved into the house, the river water rose precipitately, invading the house and filling it, to the stunning height of four feet. The steel structure was unaffected and the superficial injury to the wood of the core proved reparable. The most serious damage was confined to furniture and draperies, wounds grievous enough, of course, and sufficient to mark the incident as historic.

The water continued to overflow the river bank on a more or less regular basis, two or three times a year. Yet since nothing over the next four decades approached the incident of 1954, that date came to be spoken of simply as the year of the flood of the century, a momentous phenomenon but one unlikely to recur in the foreseeable future.

Once again, the conclusion proved presumptuous. In July of 1996 a rainfall of biblical measure laid waste the entire Fox River valley and neighboring areas. Eighteen inches fell on nearby Aurora in a 24-

hour period, the rain descending so rapidly and steadily that no one could reach the Farnsworth House in time to save its contents. Palumbo was not in residence at the time. The water broke two of the window walls and rose in the interior to a height of 58 inches. The furniture was seriously damaged or destroyed outright. Several art works were lost. Worst of all, the wood of the core was soaked and warped beyond repair. The cost of the disaster ran to more than half a million dollars, roughly four times the price Palumbo had paid for the house, seven times what Farnsworth had given for it.

Fortunately, the structure remained intact, as it had in 1954, testimony once again to the solidity of the design. Lohan was assigned responsibility a second time for the needed restoration, which now

Top: The close proximity of the Farnsworth House to the Fox River is more readily apparent in winter.

Bottom: The site flooded during construction.

25

Right: The flood of 1996 left the Farnsworth House standing in ten feet of water.

Far right: The interior soon after the flood water receded and the debris had been removed. The high-water mark is clearly visible on the wood panelling.

Below right: The core and furnishings before the 1996 flood and restoration. Note the brownish discoloration of the primavera wood of the core.

Opposite: The main sitting area today with the primavera veneer restored to its original blonde hue.

included the replacement of the two glass walls and the construction of an entirely new framework for the core. The new primavera, now in place, will surprise people who have visited the house only in recent years or who know it mostly through old color photographs. Examination of concealed surfaces of the original core revealed a color more nearly blonde than the familiarly recognized hue that had grown sanguine after years of oiling. The new wood has been coated with a waterproof varnish akin to the finish used on boat hulls. Since the primavera panels are now attached to their frame by clips rather than fixed by screws, they can be removed quickly and literally stored atop the core.

Quite evidently, the current strategy is defensive, based on a revised conviction that "flood of the century" is not only a cliché but an inaccurate one. Yet another flood occurred in February of 1997, rising within the interior of the house to the height of a foot, damaging nothing of consequence since the house was still empty following the 1996 misery, but suggesting strongly to everyone that flooding in

the 1990s is occurring at an increased rate all along the river valley. The consensus is that a great deal of land exurban to Chicago has been built up and paved over by new developments. Water has less place to drain than in the old days and more reason to rise and stay risen for a daunting period of time.

Given this melancholy but credible hypothesis, it is obviously not enough for the owners and administrators of the Farnsworth House to continue to react passively by enduring the caprices of nature and letting it go at that. Indeed, several proposals have come forth, all meant to protect against anticipated future depredations. One notion is to build berms, or levees, around the house, another, to move the entire structure to a presumably safer location. Neither solution has much to recommend it, since both would isolate the house from the very natural setting with which it is historically interdependent. Another suggestion has been to install beneath the footings hydraulic jacks that could, when activated by rising waters, elevate the whole house above the flood. Such a plan, although

hugely expensive, continues to receive serious study. Meanwhile, now that the house is open to the public, the Palumbos have assembled a cadre of workers who live nearby and who, on a moment's notice, day or night, are prepared to access the building, demount the primavera panels, store them atop the core, and carry any and all movable furnishings to a safe location.

26

The Farnsworth House and the Larger Public

During the 1970s Edith Farnsworth retired from practice and moved to a villa she owned in Italy near Florence. Fluent in Italian, she occupied herself with translations of poetry, especially that of Eugenio Montale, winner of the Nobel Prize in Literature in 1975. She did that surpassingly well, the way she did everything—providing it was more nearly professional than personal. Peter Palumbo remembers visiting her and listening to her as she recited verse to him with eloquence and unflagging intensity.

She died at the age of 74, in 1977. The house in Plano was lost to her, and for all purposes, she to it. Yet as surely as it is first and foremost a preeminent entry in the catalogue of the man who designed it, Mies van der Rohe, it continues through the decades to bear her name. Peter Palumbo has never referred to it any other way than the Farnsworth House. He and his wife, moreover, have

Above: Hayat and Peter Palumbo at the house in 1997.

Top right: Mies (center) on the deck during construction.

Opposite: The north elevation by daylight.

recognized that it finally belongs to a larger community, having earned its reputation as one of the legendary works in the history of modern architecture.

Among Edith Farnsworth's livelier memories was of a day when, having failed to draw the drapes on the eastern wall, she emerged scantily clad from her bathroom, only to see a small crowd of uninvited Japanese tourists on the lawn, cameras at the ready. They were, she recalled, scrutinizing the building rather than her, although it was the kind of experience that helped her sustain and rationalize her distaste for the building and its maker.

The Palumbos, free of such embarrassing recollections and unqualifiedly committed to the place, have figuratively pulled back the drapes on all four walls and opened the Farnsworth House to the world. People of all lands and callings, the scholars and the curious, believers and non-believers, other architects and other lovers of the building art, are at last in a position to visit the house at their leisure and see for themselves what has prompted fifty years of endless discussion, admiring and argumentative, about a great architect and his rare and remarkable client.

The house, after all, survived both of them. Even as it ensures them a place in history, it remains the object we finally and invariably fix upon. Its unelaborated simplicity marks it true to the idiom of its time, the mid-twentieth century, yet it is no less eloquent an example of the clarity, moderation and

exactitude associated since ancient times with classical expression in the arts. The image of the antique temple is immanent in the long thrust of the structure and the serene balance of vertical column row to horizontal roof. Even the elevation of the floor above the ground recalls the classical podium, while the terrace is a reprise of the stylobate, the temple entry stair. This double identity of contemporary feature and ancient form—illuminated by Mies's unique gifts—contributes to an air of timelessness that he himself sought to achieve in his own work.

Appropriately, the last word belongs to him:

"I remember seeing many old buildings in my home town when I was young," he once remarked. "They were mostly very simple, but very clear. I was impressed by the strength of these buildings. They did not belong to any epoch; they had been there for a thousand years and were still impressive, and nothing could change that. All the great styles passed, but they were still there. They didn't lose anything and they were still as good as on the day they were built."

Chronology

1938	Mies emigrates to the United States and settles in Chicago
1939	Edith Farnsworth graduates from Northwestern University Medical School
1945	Mies and Dr. Farnsworth meet at a dinner party
1946	Basic Farnsworth House design is fixed
	Philip Johnson comes to Chicago to gather material for exhibition
1947	Exhibition of Mies van der Rohe's work at the Museum of Modern Art
1949	Dr. Farnsworth receives an inheritance enabling construction to begin
	Philip Johnson's Glass House is finished
1951	Farnsworth House is completed
	Mies files suit against Edith Farnsworth; Dr. Farnsworth countersues
1953	"The Threat to the Next America" is published in *House Beautiful*
	Lawsuit is settled in Mies's favor
1954	River floods house to an interior height of 58 inches
1962	Peter Palumbo commissions Mies to design London office building
1968	Peter Palumbo inquires about Mies designing a house for him
	He calls Dr. Farnsworth regarding sale of house
1969	Death of Mies van der Rohe
1971	Dr. Farnsworth vacates house
1972	Peter Palumbo employs Dirk Lohan to renovate house and moves in
1977	Edith Farnsworth dies
1996	Great flood; house is seriously damaged
1997	House is restored and opened to public

Dimensions of the House

Length of interior of house, 77 feet; width, 28 feet (2156 sq. ft.)

Length of attached deck, 55 feet; width, 22 feet (1210 sq. ft.)

Floor level of house, 5 feet above ground; of deck, 2 feet above ground

Interior height of house: 9 feet 6 inches

Four supports on both long sides spaced 22 feet apart;
floor and roof cantilevered 5 feet 6 inches on either end of outermost piers

Fascias of both roof and floor slabs, 1 foot 3 inches wide

Window walls in glass 1/4 inch thick,
length of panes between columns, 10 feet 6 inches

Seven-foot-wide entrance is off center by one foot toward south walls

Floor module, 2 feet 9 inches long, 2 feet wide

Core, 24 feet 6 inches long, 12 feet wide

Twelve-foot-wide space on south for parlor area,
4-foot-wide space on north for kitchen area,
17-foot-wide space for dining area, 12-foot-wide space for sleeping area

Storage cabinet, 6 feet high, 12 feet long, 2 feet 2 inches deep

Further Reading

Architecture in Detail. *Farnsworth House: Mies van der Rohe.* Text by Adrian Gale. London: Phaidon Press, 1997.

Blaser, Werner. *Mies van der Rohe: The Art of Structure.* 6th revised edition. Boston: Birkhauser, 1997.

Cohen, Jean-Louis. *Mies van der Rohe.* Translated by Maggie Rosengarten. London: Chapman & Hall, 1996.

Global Architecture 27. *Mies van der Rohe: Farnsworth House, Plano, Illinois, 1945-1950.* Edited and photographed by Yukio Futagawa, text by Ludwig Glaeser. Tokyo: A.D.A. EDITA, 1994. OP

Global Architecture Detail. *Mies van der Rohe: Farnsworth House, Plano, Illinois, 1945-1950.* Text by Dirk Lohan. Tokyo: A.D.A. EDITA, 1976. OP

Guardini, Romano. *Letters from Lake Como: Explorations in Technology and the Human Race.* Translated by Geoffrey W. Bromiley. Grand Rapids: Wm. B. Eerdmans, 1994. OP

Hilberseimer, Ludwig. *Mies van der Rohe.* Chicago: Paul Theobald and Company, 1956. OP

Johnson, Philip. *Mies van der Rohe.* New York: Museum of Modern Art, 1947. Reprinted 1953, 1979. OP

Museum of Modern Art. *Mies van der Rohe Archive, Volume 13.* Edited by Franz Schulze and George Danforth. New York: Garland Publishing, 1989.

Neumeyer, Fritz. *The Artless Word: Mies van der Rohe on the Building Art.* Translated by Mark Jarzombek. Cambridge: MIT Press, 1991.

Schulze, Franz. *Mies van der Rohe: A Critical Biography.* Chicago: University of Chicago Press, 1985.

Tegethoff, Wolf. *Mies van der Rohe: The Villas and Country Houses.* Translated by Russell M. Stockman. Cambridge: MIT Press, 1985. OP

Photography Credits

Tom Blanchard (flood) 26

Werner Blaser 25

Chicago Historical Society, Hedrich-Blessing (Crown Hall) 10, (entrance) 13, 19, 20, 28

Howard Dearstyne (Tugendhat House) 9

Alexandre Georges (Glass House) 4

Myron Goldsmith (painted steel frame) 16

Ogden Hannaford (Mies supervising the masons) 17

Hedrich-Blessing 3, 4, 6, 26

David Hirsch (National Gallery) 10

Karen Hirsch (Palumbos) 28

House Beautiful, The Hearst Corporation (title page of article) 19

Barbara Karant 22

Len Koroski (interior with high-water mark) 26

George Lambros cover, 2, 5, 7, (Farnsworth House) 10, 11, (deck) 15, 23, 24, 27, 29

Dirk Lohan (wide-flange) 17

Newberry Library, Edith Farnsworth (Farnsworth House with screened-in deck) 15, (bridge) 20

Bernard Newman (Mies) 3, 10

Northwestern Memorial Hospital Archives (Dr. Farnsworth) 12

Franz Schulze (Mies) 8

C. W. Tuer (flooding of construction site) 25

Y. C. Wong (hot water pipes) 16

All others: Lohan Associates Archives